CLIL Readers

Audio available

Wild animals

written by
Virginia R. Mitchell

Richmond

Tigers have long tails.

They have orange and black stripes.

Lions have big teeth.
They have brown fur.

Giraffes have long necks.

They can eat from tall trees.

Elephants have big ears and a trunk.
They are very strong.

Zebras can run.

They have black and white stripes.

Hippos can swim and run.
They have small ears and short legs.

Eagles can fly.
They have brown feathers.

Monkeys can climb trees.
They have long tails.

Penguins can swim.

They have white, black and yellow feathers.

10

Polar bears can walk on ice.
They have white fur.

Whales can swim.

They are enormous!

Dolphins can jump.
They have shiny skin.

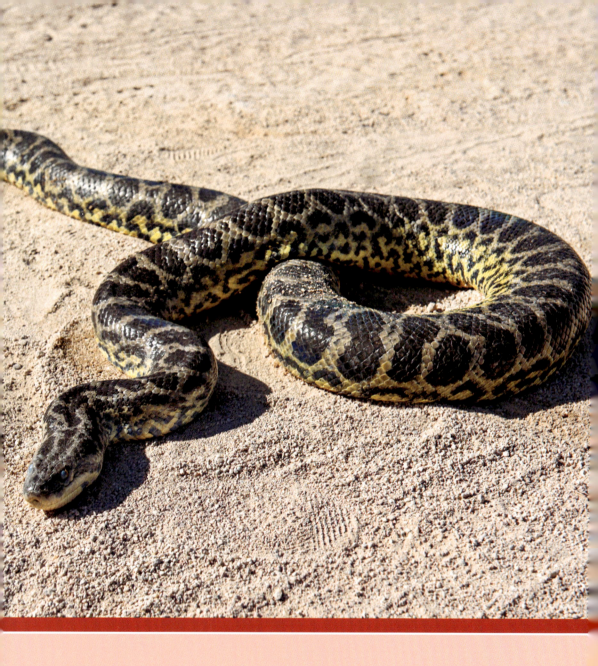

Snakes are scary.

They have long bodies.

Crocodiles are very dangerous.
They have a big mouth!

There are a lot of amazing animals.
Which one is your favourite?